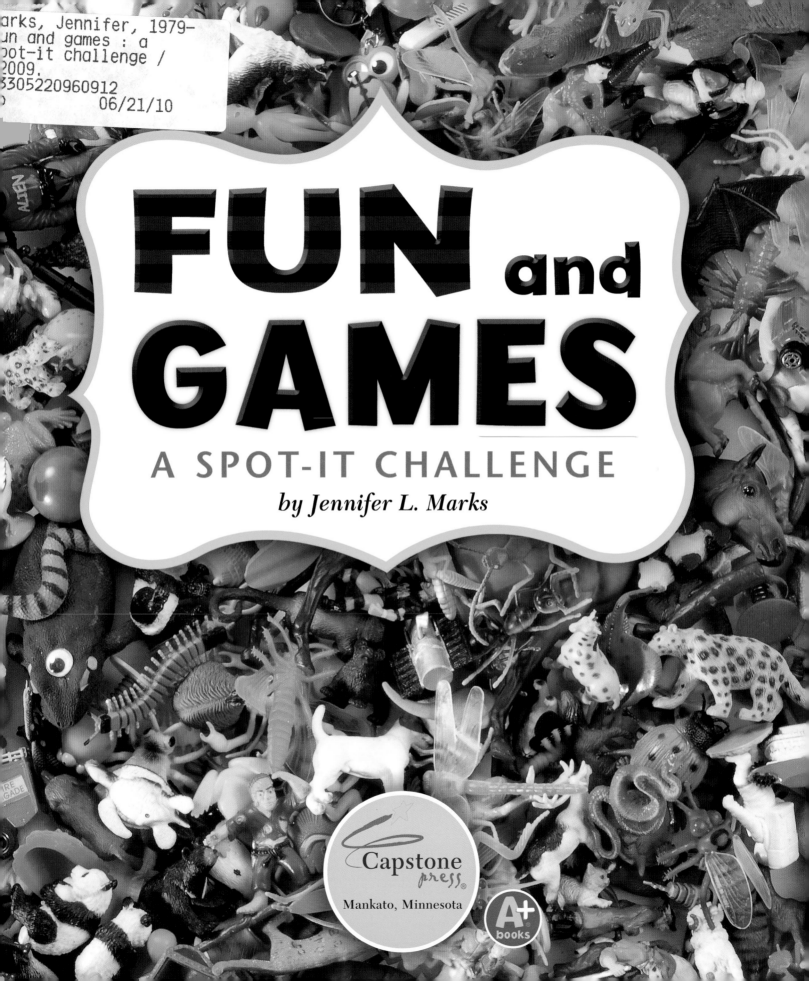

FUN and GAMES

A SPOT-IT CHALLENGE

by Jennifer L. Marks

Capstone press®

Mankato, Minnesota

A+ books

A+ Books are published by Capstone Press,
151 Good Counsel Drive, P.O. Box 669, Mankato, Minnesota 56002.
www.capstonepress.com

1 2 3 4 5 6 14 13 12 11 10 09

Library of Congress Cataloging-in-Publication Data
Marks, Jennifer L., 1979–
    Fun and games : a spot-it challenge / by Jennifer L. Marks.
    p. cm. — (A+ books. Spot it)
    Includes bibliographical references.
    Summary: "Simple text invites the reader to find items hidden in children's-game themed
photographs" — Provided by publisher.
    ISBN-13: 978-1-4296-2220-2 (hardcover)
    ISBN-10: 1-4296-2220-2 (hardcover)
    1. Games—Juvenile literature. 2. Picture puzzles —Juvenile literature. I. Title. II. Series.
GV1203.M3485 2009
793.73 — dc22   2008047248

Credits
Juliette Peters, set designer
Len Epstein, illustrator
All photos by Capstone Press Photo Studio

Note to Parents, Teachers, and Librarians
Spot It is an interactive series that supports literacy development and reading enjoyment. Readers
utilize visual discrimination skills to find objects among fun-to-peruse photographs with busy
backgrounds. Readers also build vocabulary through thematic groupings, develop visual memory
ability through repeated readings, and improve strategic and associative thinking skills by
experimenting with different visual search methods.

The author dedicates this book to the Minnesota Companion Rabbit Society, a non-profit, volunteer-based
organization that works hard to find new homes for shelter bunnies.

092009
005605R

Table of Contents

4

Step Right Up

Can you spot . . .

- a blue bunny?
- four bowling pins?
- a yo-yo?
- a puppy?
- a helicopter?
- a handkerchief?

Does This Bug You?

Can you spot . . .

- a football?
- two happy flowers?
- a garden tool?
- a fish?
- three red mushrooms?
- a treasure chest?

7

Just Playin'

Can you spot . . .

- two baseball bats?
- a pineapple?
- a first prize?
- a red balloon?
- a taxicab?
- a police car?

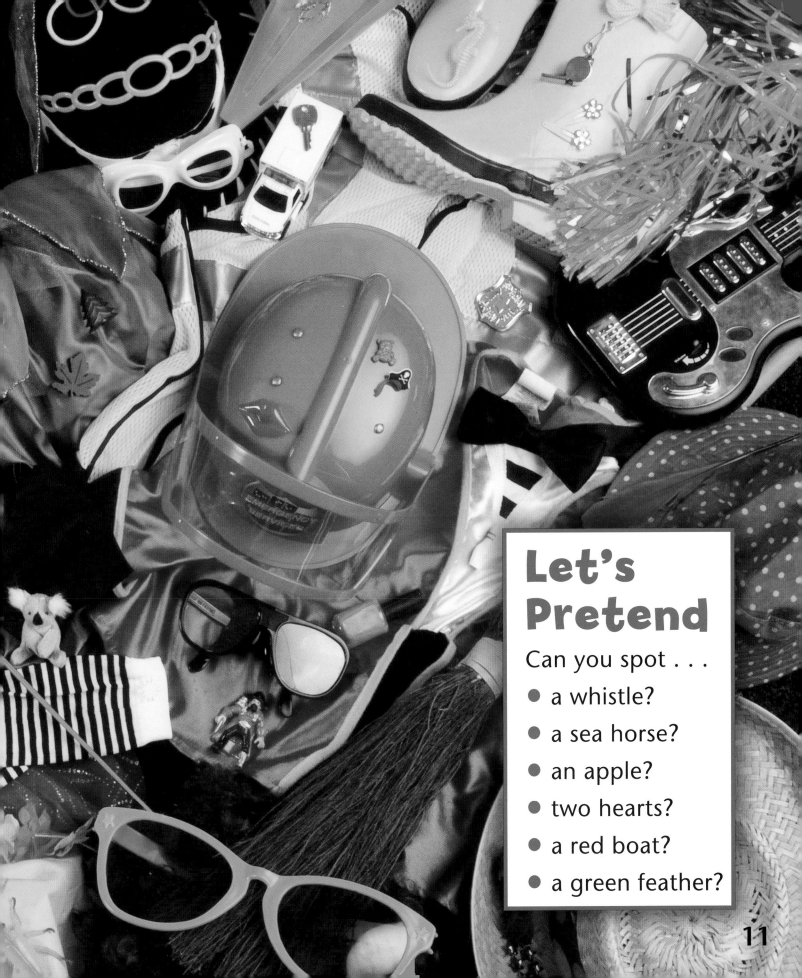

Let's Pretend

Can you spot . . .
- a whistle?
- a sea horse?
- an apple?
- two hearts?
- a red boat?
- a green feather?

Vid Kid

Can you spot . . .

- a bike?
- an ice cream cone?
- a baseball glove?
- two apple cores?
- a blue "X"?
- an upside-down tree?

Hocus Pocus

Can you spot . . .
- a flying bird?
- a fire truck?
- a tiny wizard?
- a pen?
- a star shadow?
- a red mitten?

15

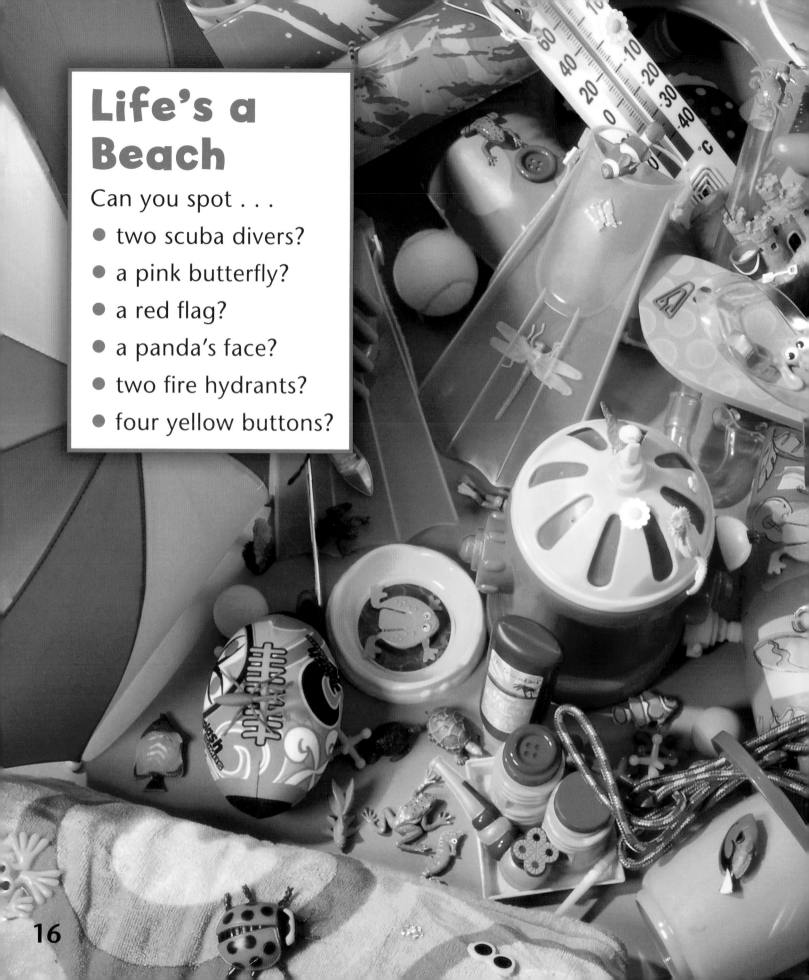

Life's a Beach

Can you spot . . .

- two scuba divers?
- a pink butterfly?
- a red flag?
- a panda's face?
- two fire hydrants?
- four yellow buttons?

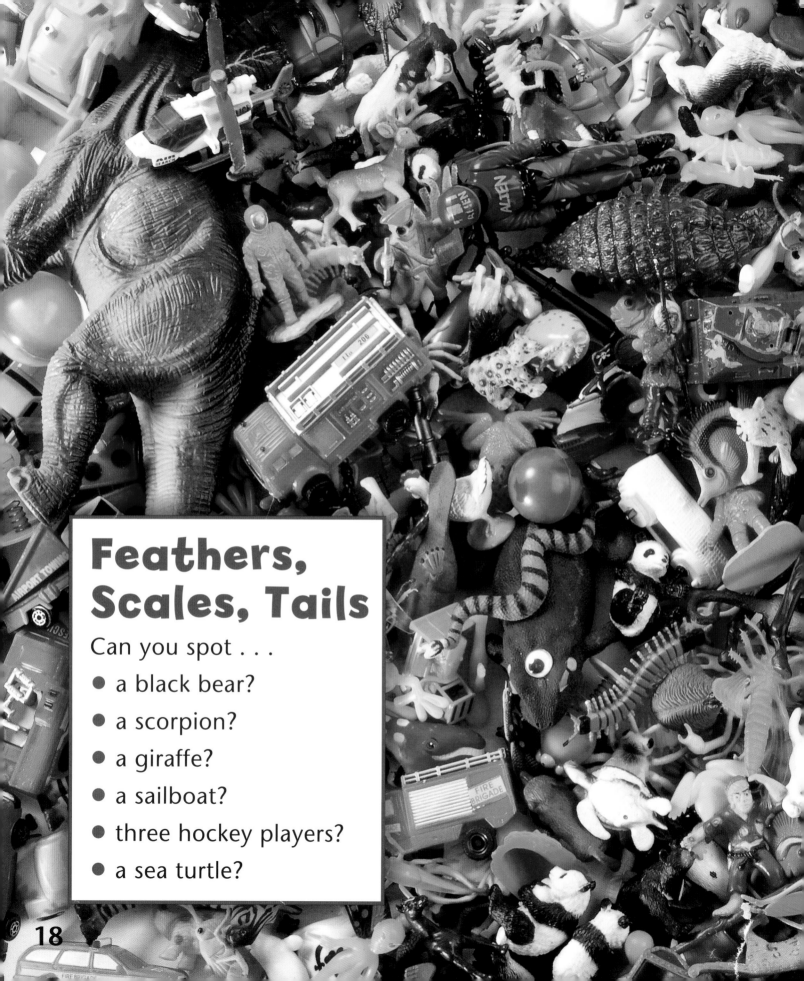

Feathers, Scales, Tails

Can you spot . . .

- a black bear?
- a scorpion?
- a giraffe?
- a sailboat?
- three hockey players?
- a sea turtle?

18

Who Needs Sleep?

Can you spot . . .

- a flamingo?
- a tack?
- two sets of keys?
- two sheep?
- two golf tees?
- a sleepy kitty?

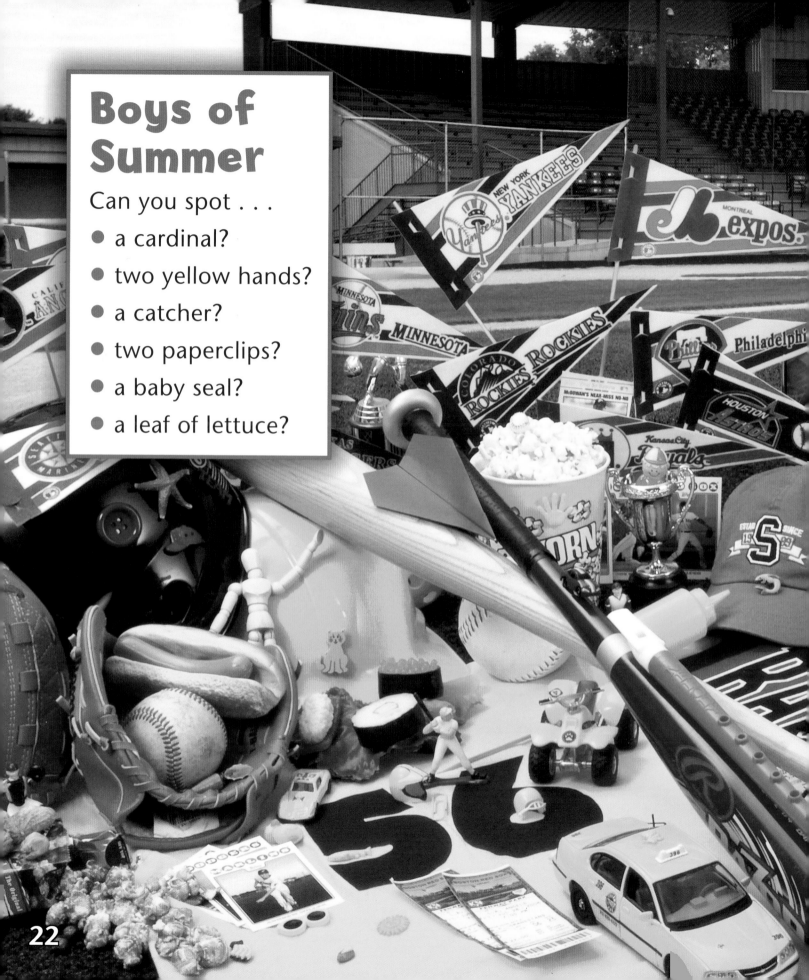

Boys of Summer

Can you spot . . .

- a cardinal?
- two yellow hands?
- a catcher?
- two paperclips?
- a baby seal?
- a leaf of lettuce?

Play with Your Food

Can you spot . . .

- a shamrock?
- a crown?
- a roller skate?
- a tractor?
- a turtle?
- a green sled?

25

On the Lawn

Can you spot . . .

- two poodles?
- a plane?
- a marble?
- two gnomes?
- a dog bone?
- a sunflower?

26

Spot Even More!

Step Right Up
Try to find a gray elephant face, a yellow bow, a clown juggling, a pink paperclip, and chattering teeth.

Does This Bug You?
See if you can spot a rabbit, a pinecone, a chair, three scorpions, a baboon, a pink tulip, and a stingray.

Just Playin'
Take another look to find an anchor, an orange button, a ghost, a bunch of grapes, and an ice cream bar.

Let's Pretend
Now find a fork, a pink comb, a jumbo diamond, a bobber, a sword, and a big pair of lips.

Vid Kid
Now spot a seagull, a stick of dynamite, two boots, cracked eyeglasses, money, and a milk carton.

Hocus Pocus
This time find a red bear, a lion, a pineapple, a scissors, a blue bear, a cherry, and the letter Y.

Life's a Beach

16

See if you can find a wind surfer, two white daisies, a pinwheel, a sand castle, and a gold necklace.

Feathers, Scales, Tails

18

Try to find a safari jeep, a black bat, a spinning top, a koala, a chicken, and a googly eye.

Who Needs Sleep?

20

Now spot a mouse, two ballet slippers, a wrench, a spatula, a dove, an orange shirt, and an apple.

Boys of Summer

22

Try to find a dalmatian, a blue car, a carrot, a cowboy hat, a bunch of bananas, and a moon.

Play with Your Food

24

Now look for an arrow, a slice of cake, a number 3, a cactus, a spiderweb, and three pieces of broccoli.

On the Lawn

26

Try to spot an astronaut, two millipedes, a walrus, a button, a turtle, and a blue jack.

Extreme Spot-It Challenge

Just can't get enough Spot-It action? Here's an extra fun-and-games challenge. Try to spot:

- two parrots
- the letter H
- a yellow airplane
- two sea stars
- a ghost
- a black housefly
- the letter Y
- a skunk
- a mermaid
- a grasshopper
- a pair of eyeglasses
- a cherry
- a monkey wearing a hat
- an orange airplane
- two plastic turtles
- a scuba diver
- two orange cones

Read More

Kidslabel. *Spot 7 Toys.* Spot 7. San Francisco: Chronicle, 2008.

Marks, Jennifer L. *Mean Machines: A Spot-It Challenge.* Spot It. Mankato, Minn.: Capstone Press, 2009.

Marzollo, Jean. *I Spy Fun House: A Book of Picture Riddles.* Scholastic, 1993.

Internet Sites

FactHound offers a safe, fun way to find educator-approved Internet sites related to this book.

Here's what you do:
1. Visit *www.facthound.com*
2. Choose your grade level.
3. Begin your search.

This book's ID number is 9781429622202.

FactHound will fetch the best sites for you!